Calculations in Chemistry: Mass, Moles, and More

A High School Chemistry Workbook with Answers

(200+ Practice Problems)

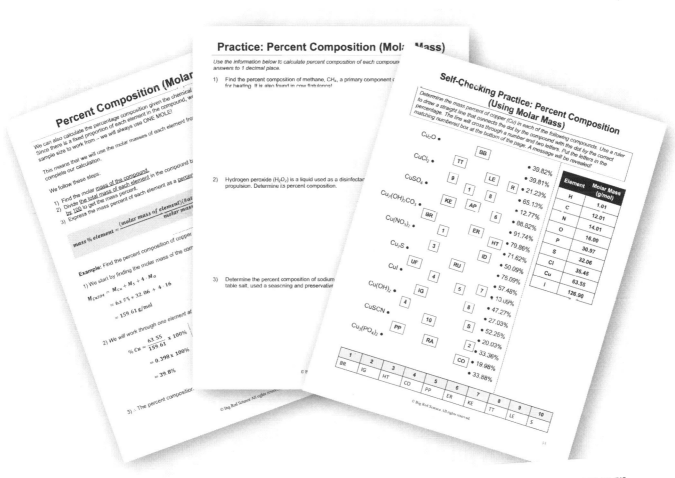

D1733738

1

Table of Contents	Page

Instructions for Use

Chemistry requires *a lot* of math. Chemists are constantly doing calculations to precisely analyze and understand the properties, interactions, and transformations of substances at the molecular level. These calculations are a *crucial skill* for any chemistry student. It is also a skill that requires *a lot of practice* to master.

The content in this workbook is designed to scaffold calculations in chemistry in a way that has students focus on one new skill at a time and then practice working with it. From there, they will do *Mixed Practice* work pages that combine everything they have learned up until that point.

The workbook should be completed in the order it is presented, as each skill builds on what was learned before. The topics included in this workbook are:

- **Significant Digits**
- **Moles, Particles, and Avogadro's Number**
- **Moles, Mass, and Molar Mass**
- **Percent Composition**
- **Empirical Formula**
- **Molecular Formula**

For each topic, this workbook includes:

Short Lessons
Each new topic begins with a short lesson. It includes an explanation of the new topic and step-by-step instructions on how to complete these new calculations.

Practice: Calculations
Each lesson is followed by at least 10 straightforward questions where students must put their new knowledge to practice. Answers are found at the end of the workbook.

Self-Checking Practice
Each section contains a self-checking practice worksheet, where students can practice their new skills to reveal a secret message or the answer to a riddle. They will know if they are right if these messages make sense! These self-checking practice worksheets are designed for students to be able to find and correct their own mistakes.

Mixed Practice
Most sections are followed by *Mixed Practice* worksheets, which combine everything that has been learned up until that point.

Significant Digits

What are Significant Digits?

Scientists do a lot of **measuring**. When scientists use equipment to measure something, they can only record a measurement as precise as the equipment is capable of.

For example, a scientist cannot measure the wingspan of the butterfly below say that it is 3.72534182936 cm. *The ruler isn't **precise** enough to make that claim!*

There is an agreement among scientists of the proper way to record measurements from any piece of equipment.

A proper measurement includes <u>all digits as read from the equipment used + 1 estimated digit</u>. We call these numbers ***significant digits***.

Using this system, we could say that the wingspan of the butterfly above is 3.7 cm. The "3" is read from the ruler and the "0.7" is our estimated digit. You might have a different estimated digit than the next person that does this measurement – that's okay!

When you're doing labs and collecting data, you must record data in this way!

When you're reading other scientists' work (including the numbers in this workbook), you must assume they recorded their data in this way as well. This assures that everyone is on the same page!

Digital Numbers

When using an electronic device (ex: an electronic balance) the measurement displayed on the screen is **assumed to have one estimated digit included**.

In fact, you'll often see the estimated digit changing rapidly, because there is fluctuation in the estimate. So *you just need to record its measurements as shown.*

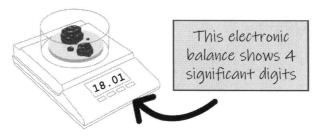

This electronic balance shows 4 significant digits

Significant Digits

What's the Point of Significant Digits?

Significant digits exist so that we can have confidence about how precise our values are when we're taking measurements and doing calculations in science.

Of course, we're not always taking measurements. Sometimes we're just working with numbers and doing calculations.

We still need to keep significant digits in mind so that we don't imply experiments were done differently!

Identifying Significant Digits

Scientists have created rules about when digits are considered to be *significant*. These rules are designed to support the idea of making accurate and precise measurements. You need to know these rules as a science student!

#	Rule	Example	Number of Significant Digits
1	All <u>non-zero</u> numbers are significant.	23.4	3
2	Zeroes <u>before</u> other numbers ("leading zeroes") are <u>not significant</u>.	0.0000<u>3</u>	1
3	Zeroes <u>after</u> other numbers ("trailing zeroes") are only significant if the number has a decimal included.	<u>2</u>000	1
		<u>2000</u>.	4
		<u>2000.00</u>	6
4	Zeroes between non-zero numbers are significant.	<u>3025</u>	4
5	Numbers that are exact counts are as precise as possible, so significant digits don't apply. We say these numbers have an infinite number of significant digits.	The class has 26 students.	infinite

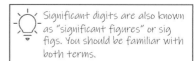
Significant digits are also known as "significant figures" or sig figs. You should be familiar with both terms.

Self-Checking Practice: Significant Digits

Take a look at each number and determine its number of significant digits. Highlight the correct answer (either Option 1 or Option 2) and place the corresponding letters in the blank spaces at the bottom of the page from 1 to 9. A message will appear!

#	Number	How many significant digits? Option 1	How many significant digits? Option 2
6	19	1 [ROBY]	2 [ELEA]
1	52 cards in a deck	Infinite [INSC]	2 [DECE]
7	0.0023	5 [HOPS]	2 [DSTO]
5	400.	3 [LUR]	1 [PON]
2	10002	2 [PETR]	5 [IENC]
8	400	1 [DISCO]	3 [MEADY]
3	1.36×10^{23}	3 [EEVEN]	26 [JUSTA]
4	21.000003	3 [EYA]	8 [FAI]
9	42.0	2 [LASH]	3 [VERY]

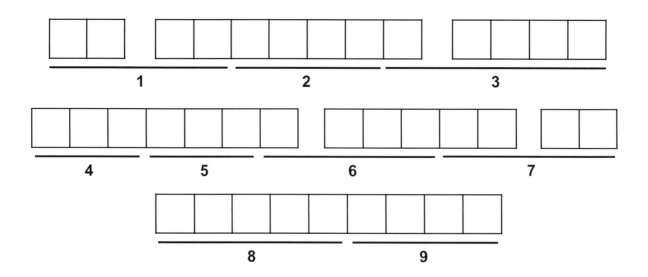

Doing Math with Significant Digits

Remember, *precision* is extremely important in science. Being precise increases the accuracy of both experimental results and theoretical predictions.

Chemistry involves a lot of calculations. Inevitably, this means that you will need to **round** your answers.

Rounding according to some <u>significant digit rules</u> keeps things consistent in our measurements and calculated quantities.

These rules matter!

They guide us how to round in a way that doesn't suggest we used a piece of equipment that was more precise than it really was.

Rules for Significant Digits in Calculations

1) Round at the **<u>end</u>** of your calculations. If you have a series of calculations to do, keep all digits in your calculator until the very end. You should only be rounding **<u>once</u>**.

2) <u>Addition and Subtraction</u>

- Round the answer to the **<u>fewest number of decimal places</u>** in the original numbers being added or subtracted.

- Example: $6.213 + 1.24 + 12.2 = 19.653$

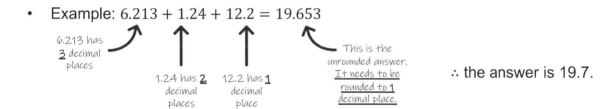

6.213 has **3** decimal places

1.24 has **2** decimal places

12.2 has **1** decimal place

This is the unrounded answer. It needs to be rounded to 1 decimal place.

∴ the answer is 19.7.

3) <u>Multiplication and Division</u>

- Determine the number of significant digits in each number in the question. Round the answer to the **<u>fewest number of significant digits</u>** among the original numbers being multiplied or divided.

Note: A dot "·" means multiplication. This is how you will typically see multiplication shown in this workbook.

- Example: $3.21 \cdot 2.4 = 7.704$

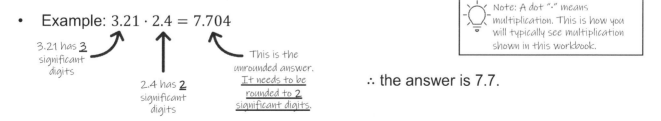

3.21 has **3** significant digits

2.4 has **2** significant digits

This is the unrounded answer. It needs to be rounded to 2 significant digits.

∴ the answer is 7.7.

Self-Checking Practice: Doing Math with Significant Digits

Answer each question below and round your result to the proper number of significant digits. Find your answer below and cross out the letter above it. Unscramble the remaining letters to find the answer to the riddle!

$60.5 \cdot 2.5 =$ _____	$9.13 + 12.1328 =$ _____
$12.3 + 4.56 =$ _____	$737.885 \div 17.9 =$ _____
$87.42 - 23.5 =$ _____	$9.50 \cdot 2.2 =$ _____
$975.12 \div 3211.3 =$ _____	$123.4 + 5678 =$ _____

what falls down but never gets hurt?

N	P	S	A	E	L	U	K	T	R	B	I
41.223	21.26	63.9	0.31	41.2	5801	150	0.30365	21	21.3	16.9	151.25

Answer: _____

WARNING: Read Before Proceeding!

Use a Scientific Calculator
Your phone is not good enough for calculations in chemistry! You should be using brackets, exponents, scientific notation, and previously stored answers regularly. Even inexpensive scientific calculators make these functions simple. **Trust the experts in chemistry education** – you will minimize silly calculation errors when you don't try to do everything on your phone!

Round at the End
To maintain accuracy and prevent cumulative errors, do all calculations without rounding until the final step. Then, round the final result to the appropriate number of significant digits.

Pay Attention to Significant Digits
Follow the rules for significant digits to express your final answer with the correct level of precision. If you check your answer and your significant digits don't match, look back at the original question and try to understand where you went wrong.

Check and Double-Check
It's always a good idea to redo your calculations for accuracy and consistency – especially when dealing with multi-step problems. A second review will help you catch any mistakes!

Pay Attention to Units
Make sure you are tracking units and including the correct units in your final answer.

Look for this Symbol
You will see this symbol throughout this workbook ▦ . It is drawing your attention to something about the calculation!

Check Your Answers
The answer to each problem is found at the back of the workbook. Do a few problems in each section and then check your answers to ensure you know what you're doing!

Be Strategic
This workbook has a lot of practice problems. If you feel like you've mastered a skill after a third of the practice problems in a section, feel free to move on! You might want to save some problems for review before a test. It's up to you!

The Mole Concept

What is a Mole?

Chemists work with atoms and molecules. These are tiny. If chemists were trying to describe how many atoms were in a certain sample of an element, they would have to use HUGE numbers all the time.

Chemists use **the mole** as a simpler way to "count" atoms, particles, and molecules.

Just like we can use a *dozen* to count 12 items, chemists use a *mole* to count a large number of particles. One mole (abbreviated as "mol") is equal to…

$$6.02 \times 10^{23}$$

This is known as Avogadro's Number, and it is the number of particles in one mole of a substance.

It's a **HUGE** number! It was named after the Italian scientist Amedeo Avogadro, who first proposed that equal volumes of gases, at the same temperature and pressure, contain the same number of particles.

Connecting Moles, Avogadro's Number, and Particles

This simple formula connects moles, Avogadro's number, and particles:

$$n = \frac{N}{N_A}$$

Number of particles *

Number of moles

Avogadro's Number
6.02×10^{23}

In this formula:

*Particles can mean atoms, ions, molecules, or formula units. A formula unit is a unit of an ionic compound, whereas a molecule is a unit of a molecular compound.

n = Number of moles
N = Number of particles
N_A = Avogadro's number (i.e. the constant 6.02×10^{23})

Note: You should also be able to rearrange this formula to solve for N and N_A:

To solve for N:	To solve for N_A:
$N = n \cdot N_A$	$N_A = \dfrac{N}{n}$

It's rare that you'll be asked to calculate Avogadro's Number, but it can happen!

The Mole Concept

Example 1: Let's say we have 8.94×10^{24} atoms of carbon in a sample of coal. How many moles of carbon do we have?

$$n = \frac{N}{N_A}$$

$$= \frac{8.95 \times 10^{24}}{6.02 \times 10^{23}}$$

$$= 14.9$$

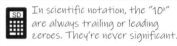

In scientific notation, the "10^x" are always trailing or leading zeroes. They're never significant.

$\therefore$ there are 14.9 moles of carbon in this sample of coal.

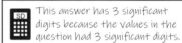

This answer has 3 significant digits because the values in the question had 3 significant digits.

Example 2: A chemist has 1.5 moles of a sample of potassium sulfide, K_2S.

a) How many particles of K_2S do they have?
b) How many total atoms do they have in the sample?

a)

$$N_{particles} = n \cdot N_A$$

$$= 1.5 \cdot 6.02 \times 10^{23}$$

$$= 9.03 \times 10^{23}$$

$\therefore$ there are 9.03×10^{23} particles of K_2S in the sample.

b) To determine the total number of *atoms* in the sample, we need to look at how many atoms are in 1 "particle" of K_2S. There are 3 total atoms: 2 potassium; 1 sulfur.

Therefore, we multiply our answer from a) by 3. This is how many total atoms exist in the sample.

$$N_{atoms} = 3 \cdot N_{particles}$$

$$= 3 \cdot 9.03 \times 10^{23}$$

$$= 2.71 \times 10^{24}$$

$\therefore$ there are 2.71×10^{24} atoms in the K_2S sample.

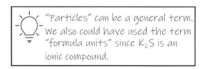

"Particles" can be a general term. We also could have used the term "formula units" since K_2S is an ionic compound.

Practice: Moles and Avogadro's Number

Part A: Use the information below to calculate the number of moles in each sample. Remember to round your final answer to the appropriate number of significant digits.

1) A sample of oxygen contains 5.67×10^{24} atoms of oxygen. How many moles are in the sample?

2) A glass of water contains 2.81×10^{23} molecules of water (H_2O). How many moles of water are in the glass?

3) If a sample of carbon contains 1.20×10^{25} atoms of carbon (C), how many moles of carbon are in the sample?

4) If an average exhaled breath contains approximately 4.5×10^{19} molecules of carbon dioxide, how many moles of CO_2 are present in one exhaled breath?

5) A 355 ml can of soda contains approximately 5.32×10^{22} molecules of carbon dioxide. How many moles of CO_2 are present in this can?

Practice: Moles and Avogadro's Number

...continued

6) In an hour of moderate exercise, a person uses about 1.87×10^{22} molecules of oxygen (O_2). Calculate the number of moles of oxygen consumed by them during this exercise period.

7) A sample of aluminum foil (Al) contains 3.13×10^{21} atoms of aluminum. How many moles are in this sample of foil?

8) A beaker of potassium hydroxide (KOH) contains 3.84×10^{20} formula units. Determine the number of moles in this beaker.

9) An iron nail contains approximately 2.71×10^{22} atoms of iron. How many moles of iron are in this nail?

10) A blimp contains 1.35×10^{30} atoms of helium (He). How many moles of helium are in the blimp?

Practice: Particles and Avogadro's Number

Part B: Use the information below to calculate the number of particles in each sample. Remember to round your final answer to the appropriate number of significant digits.

1) How many formula units are in 1.2 moles of sodium chloride (NaCl)?

2) Calculate the number of atoms in 2.5 moles of carbon (C).

3) Determine the number of molecules in 0.75 moles of oxygen gas (O_2).

4) How many molecules are in 0.25 moles of carbon dioxide gas (CO_2)?

5) How many atoms are in 0.25 moles of carbon dioxide gas (CO_2)?

Practice: Particles and Avogadro's Number

...continued

6) Calculate the number of formula units in 2.3 moles of magnesium chloride ($MgCl_2$).

7) Calculate the number of chloride ions in 2.3 moles of magnesium chloride ($MgCl_2$).

8) Determine the number of atoms in 0.40 moles of sulfur (S).

9) Calculate the number of molecules in 2.5 moles of methane gas (CH_4).

10) How many carbon atoms are in 0.36 moles of ethanol (C_2H_5OH)?

Self-Checking Practice:
Moles, Particles, and Avogadro's Number

You can find me in the alkali metals and the alkaline earth metals, but you won't find me in the transition metals. Who am I?

T	Calculate the number of atoms in 3.00 moles of iron (Fe).
E	How many atoms are present in 8.00 moles of sulfur dioxide (SO_2)?
E	How many moles is 1.2×10^{22} atoms of carbon?
T	Calculate the number of moles present in a sample of 1.80×10^{24} molecules of hydrogen (H_2)?
L	Find the number of molecules in 13.8 mol of water.
R	How many formula units are in 1.50 moles of $Ba(NO_3)_2$?
T	Calculate the number of moles present in a sample that contains 5.38×10^{17} formula units of $CaBr_2$.
K	How many molecules are in 1.00 mole of carbon monoxide (CO)?
H	Find the number of moles present in a sample of carbon dioxide (CO_2) containing 9.90×10^{23} atoms.
E	How many moles makes up a sample of 1.51×10^{24} atoms of neon gas (Ne)?

8.94×10^{-7}	1.64	0.20	8.31×10^{24}	1.44×10^{25}	2.99	1.81×10^{24}	2.51	9.03×10^{23}	6.02×10^{23}

Moles, Mass, and Molar Mass

Most people are familiar with the idea of **mass**. In chemistry, mass is an important property of matter, representing how much of a substance is present. It's measured using a balance and recorded with the unit of **grams (g)**.

This sample of carbon has a mass of 18.01 g.

Molar mass, on the other hand, refers to the *mass of one mole of a substance* and is expressed in **grams per mole (g/mol)**. The molar mass of each element can be found using the periodic table.

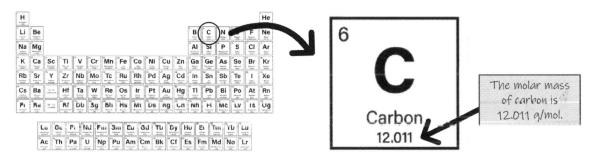

The molar mass of carbon is 12.011 g/mol.

When calculating the molar mass of a compound, we need to examine how many atoms of each element are present and do a quick calculation.

Example: Let's calculate the molar mass of water (H_2O).

Water contains 2 hydrogen atoms and 1 oxygen atom. Find H and O on the periodic table and take note of their molar masses.

M_H = 1.01 g/mol
M_O = 16.00 g/mol

In high school chemistry, it's pretty typical to round molar masses to 2 decimal places. This is what we will do in this workbook.

For each element in the compound, we need to multiply its molar mass by the number of atoms of that element in the molecule. Then, we add up these values to get the molar mass of the entire molecule.

There are 2 H atoms in H_2O, so: M_H = 2 · 1.01 = <u>2.02</u>

There is 1 O atom in H_2O, so: M_O = 1 · 16.00 = <u>16.00</u>

M_{H2O} = 2.02 + 16.00 = **<u>18.02 g/mol</u>**

∴ the molar mass of water is 18.02 g/mol.

Self-Checking Practice: Calculating Molar Mass

Calculate the molar mass of each compound and use your answers to guide you through the maze and pick up symbols along the way. Use the decoder to reveal a secret word!

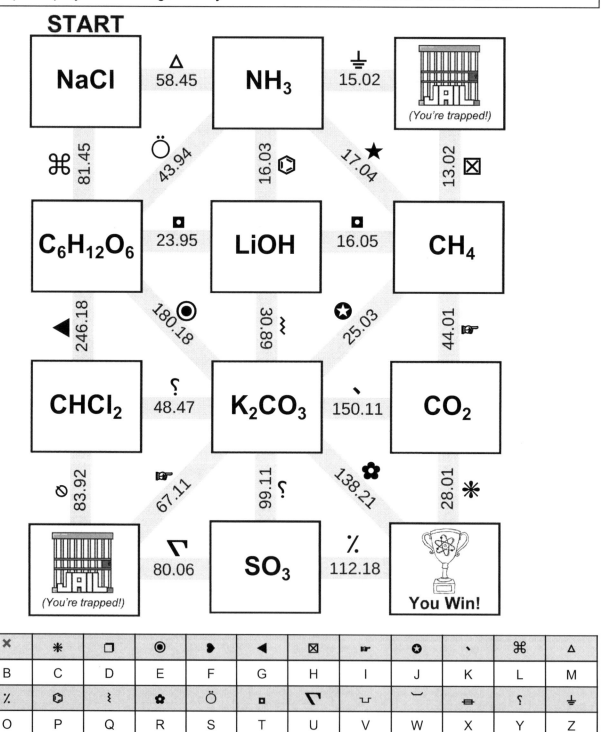

Decoder

★	✕	✳	❑	◉	◗	◀	⊠	☛	✪	`	⌘	△
A	B	C	D	E	F	G	H	I	J	K	L	M
∅	⁒	⬡	⌇	✿	Ö	▫	⌐	⊔	⌣	⊟	¿	⚊
N	O	P	Q	R	S	T	U	V	W	X	Y	Z

Moles, Mass, and Molar Mass

Connecting Moles, Mass, and Molar Mass

This simple formula connects moles, mass, and molar mass:

$$M = \frac{m}{n}$$

Molar mass   Mass   Number of moles

<u>In this formula</u>:

m = mass (in g)
n = number of moles (in mol)
M = molar mass (in g/mol)

Note: You should also be able to rearrange this formula to solve for m and n.

To solve for m:	To solve for n:
$m = M \cdot n$	$n = \dfrac{m}{M}$

Example 1: In the diagram below, we have 18.01 g of carbon. How many moles of carbon are in this sample?

This sample of carbon has a mass of 18.01 g.

$$n = \frac{m}{M}$$

$$= \frac{18.01}{12.01}$$

$$= 1.500 \; moles$$

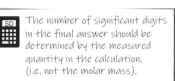

The number of significant digits in the final answer should be determined by the measured quantity in the calculation. (i.e. not the molar mass).

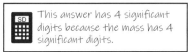

This answer has 4 significant digits because the mass has 4 significant digits.

∴ there are 1.500 moles of carbon in this sample.

Moles, Mass, and Molar Mass

Example 2: A chemist has 5.25 moles of a sample of copper (II) chloride ($CuCl_2$). What is the mass of the sample?

$$m = M \cdot n$$

First, we need to calculate the molar mass of $CuCl_2$.

$$M_{CuCl2} = M_{Cu} + 2 \cdot M_{Cl}$$

$$= 63.55 + 2 \cdot 35.5$$

$$= 134.55 \, g/mol$$

Next, we need to use the molar mass to calculate the mass.

$$m = M \cdot n$$

$$= 134.55 \cdot 5.25$$

$$= 706$$

 This answer has 3 significant digits because the mass has 3 significant digits. Remember, molar mass doesn't impact significant digits.

∴ there are 706 g of $CuCl_2$ in this sample.

Example 3: A chemist has a sample of an unknown element. There are 0.07125 moles and it has a mass of 13.9 g. Determine the molar mass and identify the element.

Element	Molar Mass (g/mol)
Magnesium	24.31
Iron	55.85
Tin	118.71
Platinum	195.09
Bismuth	208.98

$$M = \frac{m}{n}$$

$$= \frac{13.9}{0.07125}$$

$$= 195$$

∴ the molar mass is 195.09 g/mol and the unknown element is platinum.

Using Conversion Triangles

The two formulas that we have used so far are very important in chemistry, and you will commonly see them shared as **conversion triangles**.

When working with any formula that contain 3 variables, it can be helpful to set them up in this triangle format. They provide a visual representation of the relationships between different units or variables, making it easier to convert between them. They can streamline calculations and help ensure accuracy for a lot of students.

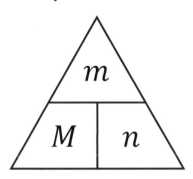 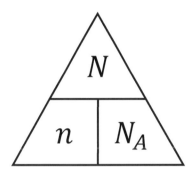

It should be noted that some teachers strongly dislike students using the triangle strategy. Often, they believe students should be able to rearrange formulas without using this visual aid as a crutch. This is a valid concern, so make sure that you are also able to rearrange formulas with ease.

Regardless of what strategy you use, *you should seek to have an understanding of why these formulas make sense.*

For example, the formula for molar mass is really easy to remember if you simply remember the units of molar mass: **g/mol**. This is the formula! Mass (g) divided by # moles gives us the mass of 1 mole (aka molar mass).

How to use the Triangle

OK, you've drawn your triangle – now how do you use it? You find the variable you're looking for and "cover it up". Look at the placement of the other two variables. If they're beside each other, that means you multiply. If one is on top of the other, then you divide (think of the horizontal line as a fraction line).

That's it!

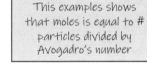

This examples shows that moles is equal to # particles divided by Avogadro's number

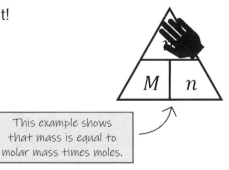

This example shows that mass is equal to molar mass times moles.

Practice: Moles, Mass, and Molar Mass

Part A: Use the information below to calculate the number of moles in each sample. Remember to round your final answer to the appropriate number of significant digits.

1)   A sample of sodium metal has a mass of 22.4 g. How many moles are in the sample?

2)   A sample of water has a mass of 235.8 g. How many moles of water are present?

3)   If a sample of potassium iodide (KI) has a mass of 32.7 g, how many moles of KI are in the sample?

4)   A tank holds a sample of argon gas that has a mass of 1319 g. How many moles of argon are in the tank?

5)   A recipe calls for a cup of sugar. The common chemical name for sugar is sucrose ($C_{12}H_{22}O_{11}$). If a particular cup of sugar weighs 202 g, how many moles of sugar are in this cup?

Practice: Moles, Mass, and Molar Mass

...continued

6) A scrunched up ball of aluminum foil has a mass of 332.8 g. How many moles are in this ball of foil?

7) A recipe calls for 75 g of table salt (NaCl). How many moles of sodium chloride are in this sample?

8) How many moles of sodium hydroxide (NaOH) are in a 12.2 g sample of the solid?

9) If a solid gold ring has a mass of 8.48 g, how many moles of gold are in this ring?

10) A sample of carbon tetrachloride (CCl_4) has a mass of 2649 g. How many moles are in this sample?

Practice: Moles, Mass, and Molar Mass

Part B: Use the information below to calculate the mass of each sample. Remember to round your final answer to the appropriate number of significant digits.

1) What is the mass of a 2.5 mol sample of carbon dioxide (CO_2)?

2) What is the mass of a 2.5 mol sample of carbon monoxide (CO)?

3) Determine the mass of 0.645 moles of sulfur dioxide (SO_2)?

4) Calculate the mass of 1.792 moles of aluminum oxide (Al_2O_3).

5) Determine the mass of 1.40 moles of sodium sulfate (Na_2SO_4).

Practice: Moles, Mass, and Molar Mass

...continued

6) What is the mass of 5.00 moles of aluminum foil?

7) What is the mass of 100. moles of silver?

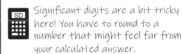

Significant digits are a bit tricky here! You have to round to a number that might feel far from your calculated answer.

8) Determine the mass of 3.87 moles of hydrogen cyanide (HCN).

9) Find the mass of 18.00 moles of calcium bromide ($CaBr_2$).

10) Calculate the mass of 0.00021 moles of platinum.

Self-Checking Practice:
Moles, Mass, and Molar Mass

Solve for the unknown given the information below. Find your answer on the next page (without units) and cross out the letter above it. The answer to the question will remain!

$n = 1.35\ mol;\ M = 24.4\ g/mol;\ \boldsymbol{m} =?$	$m\ = 119.5\ g;\ n = 5.2\ mol;\ \boldsymbol{M} =?$
$m\ = 4.5\ g;\ M = 12.01;\ \boldsymbol{n} =?$	$n = 3.30\ mol;\ M = 226\ g/mol;\ \boldsymbol{m} =?$
$m\ = 9.01\ g;\ n = 0.50\ mol;\ \boldsymbol{M} =?$	$m\ = 0.061\ g;\ M = 35.45 g/mol;\ \boldsymbol{n} =?$
$n = 2.233\ mol;\ M = 125.39\ g/mol;\ \boldsymbol{m} =?$	$m\ = 2.0\ g;\ n = 0.0268\ mol;\ \boldsymbol{M} =?$
$m\ = 0.015\ g;\ M = 64.06\ g/mol;\ \boldsymbol{n} =?$	$m\ = 1.0\ g;\ n = 0.0179\ mol;\ \boldsymbol{M} =?$
$m\ = 52.1\ g;\ M = 180.2\ g/mol;\ \boldsymbol{n} =?$	$n = 0.050\ mol;\ M = 169.4\ g/mol;\ \boldsymbol{m} =?$

Self-Checking Practice:
Moles, Mass, and Molar Mass

What kind of table has no legs?

A	R	P	S	Y	I	E	L	R	E
18	8.47	0.032	280.0	746	75	82	32.9	0.98	23

I	O	S	M	D	H	I	W	L	C
0.0099	30.4	56	0.00023	31	0.0017	49.1	0.37	0.289	62.5

Answer: _____

Mixed Practice
Avogadro's Number, Particles, Moles, Molar Mass, Mass

Use the information below to find the unknown variable in each question. Remember to round your final answer to the appropriate number of significant digits.

1) A chemistry student has 1.8 moles of iron (III) oxide (Fe_2O_3). What is the mass of iron (III) oxide in grams?

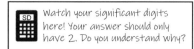

Watch your significant digits here! Your answer should only have 2. Do you understand why?

2) How many moles make up a sample of 4.514×10^{15} atoms of platinum?

3) How many atoms are found in a spoon that contains 5.14×10^{22} formula units of table salt (sodium chloride; NaCl)?

4) A necklace is just over 9 g and contains 5.2×10^{22} silver atoms. How many moles of silver are in this necklace?

5) How many molecules are present in a sample of 0.026 moles of caffeine ($C_8H_{10}N_4O_2$)?

Mixed Practice
Avogadro's Number, Particles, Moles, Molar Mass, Mass

...continued

6) Naphtalene is an organic compound responsible for the pungent smell of moth balls. If 0.00109101 moles of naphthalene has a mass of 0.1399, what is the molar mass of the compound?

7) What is the mass of a sample of solid sodium hydroxide (NaOH)pellets that contains 3.30 moles?

8) Annabelle has a box of baking soda (sodium bicarbonate; $NaHCO_3$) that has a mass of 255 g. How many moles of baking soda are present in the box?

9) What is the molar mass of nicotine ($C_{10}H_{14}N_2$)?

10) Find the mass of 2.3 moles of zinc needed for a chemical reaction.

Percent Composition

Percent composition is an important concept in chemistry that tells us the relative amounts of each element present in a compound. It helps us understand what substances are made of by showing the proportion of each element's mass compared to the total mass of the compound.

It is sometimes referred to as **mass percent** or **percentage composition**, so if you see these terms in your chemistry education, remember that they mean the same thing. This workbook uses *mass percent* when talking about the percent of one element in a compound.

The elements in a chemical compound are always present in the <u>same proportions by mass</u>. For example, the mass percent of hydrogen in water is always 11.2% and the mass percent of oxygen in water is always 88.8%.

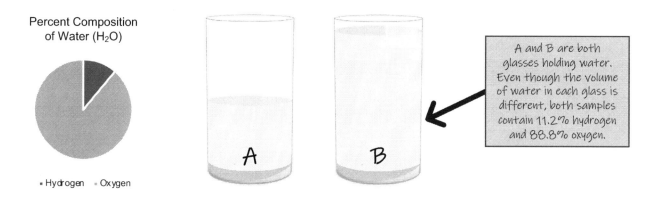

Percent Composition of Water (H₂O)

- Hydrogen   - Oxygen

A and B are both glasses holding water. Even though the volume of water in each glass is different, both samples contain 11.2% hydrogen and 88.8% oxygen.

It is possible to have *different compounds* made up of *difference amounts* of the *same elements*.

For example, carbon monoxide (CO) and carbon dioxide (CO_2) are both made of carbon and oxygen but each compound has unique properties:

Carbon dioxide	Carbon monoxide
• **27.29% carbon and 72.71% oxygen** • *A natural component of Earth's atmosphere* • *Produced by various processes including cellular respiration, volcanic eruptions, and combustion of organic matter (both naturally and during industrial processes).*	• **42.85% carbon and 57.15% oxygen** • *Highly toxic* • *Bonds to hemoglobin in blood, preventing O_2 from being transported to the body's cells* • *Often produced from industrial processes and vehicle exhausts.*
$\ddot{O}=C=\ddot{O}$	$:C\equiv O:$

Calculating percentage composition will help us to eventually calculate the chemical formulas of unknown compounds.

Percent Composition (Using Samples)

To calculate percent composition when given information about a sample, we follow these steps:

1) Divide the <u>mass of each element</u> in a compound by the <u>total mass</u> of the compound.
2) Multiply each result by <u>100%</u> to express it as a percentage.

$$mass\ \%\ of\ element = \frac{mass\ of\ element}{mass\ of\ compound} \times 100\%$$

Example: A compound is made up of 4 elements: aluminum, carbon, hydrogen, and oxygen. The table below shows the breakdown of masses in a 50.0 g sample of the compound:

Element	Mass (g)
Aluminum (Al)	6.60
Carbon (C)	17.7
Hydrogen (H)	2.2
Oxygen (O)	23.5

We will work through one element at a time:

$\% Al = \dfrac{6.60}{50.0} \times 100\%$

$= 0.132 \times 100\%$

$= 13.2\%$

$\% C = \dfrac{17.7}{50.0} \times 100\%$

$= 0.354 \times 100\%$

$= 35.4\%$

$\% H = \dfrac{2.2}{50.0} \times 100\%$

$= 0.044 \times 100\%$

$= 4.4\%$

$\% O = \dfrac{23.5}{50.0} \times 100\%$

$= 0.47 \times 100\%$

$= 47\%$

∴The compound is composed of 13.2% Al, 35.4% C, 4.4% H, and 47% O.

In the above calculations, you'll notice that the percentages add up to 100%. Hopefully this makes sense to you, as the percentages represent the compound's entire composition. Every element should be fully accounted for! ***If you find that your percentages don't quite add up to 100%, it might be due to small differences because of rounding.*** This often happens when maintaining the rules for significant digits and isn't a big deal.

You might have already noticed that there is a second option to calculate the mass percent of the final element in a compound. You can simply subtract all of the other percentages from 100%, and your answer will be the mass percent of the final element.

For example: $\% O = 100 - (13.2 + 35.4 + 4.4)$

$= 47\%$

Practice: Percent Composition (Samples)

Use the information below to answer each percent composition problem.

1) A compound containing copper and bromine has a mass of 134 g. The mass of copper in the compound is 38.1 g. Determine the percent composition of the compound.

Cu	%
Br	%

2) A compound is made up of chlorine and hydrogen. If its mass is 17 g and the mass of hydrogen in the compound is 0.51 g, what is the percent composition of the compound?

H	%
Cl	%

3) A 12.00 g sample of an ionic compound contains 6.294 g of potassium and 5.706 g of chlorine. Determine the compound's percent composition.

K	%
Cl	%

Practice: Percent Composition (Samples)

...continued

4) A sample of iron (II) phosphate has a mass of 221.5 g. The iron component is 103.7 g, the phosphorus component is 38.30 g, and the oxygen component is 79.50 g. What is the percent composition of the compound?

Fe	%
P	%
O	%

5) A sample of nickel, sulfur, and oxygen has a mass of 58.0 g. Nickel makes up 16.8 g of the mass and sulfur makes up 13.7 g. What mass of the compound is oxygen? What is the mass percent of oxygen in the compound?

O	g
O	%

6) A compound contains 162 g of magnesium, 80.0 g of carbon, and 321 g of oxygen. Determine the percent composition of the compound.

Mg	%
C	%
O	%

Practice: Percent Composition (Samples)

...continued

7) The mass of a sample of a molecular compound is 19.6 g. Nitrogen makes up 16.1 g of the sample and hydrogen makes up 3.5 g. What is the mass percent of nitrogen in the sample?

N	%

8) A compound contains 45.77 g of zinc and 22.44 g of sulfur. What is the percent composition of the compound?

Zn	%
S	%

9) A mystery compound contains carbon, hydrogen, and chlorine. If the sample has a mass of 0.0704 g and the the combined mass of carbon and hydrogen in the compound is 0.00768 g. What is the mass percent of chlorine in this compound?

Cl	%

Practice: Percent Composition (Samples)

…continued

10) The percent composition of dinitrogen pentoxide is: 25.9% nitrogen and 74.1% oxygen. What mass of nitrogen would be present in a 235 g sample of N_2O_5?

 Convert the percentage of N to a decimal and multiply it by the total mass of the sample. This will give you the mass of the N portion of the compound.

N		g

11) The percent composition of magnesium nitrate is 16.4% magnesium, 18.9% nitrogen, and 64.7% oxygen. What is the mass of magnesium in a 45 g sample of $Mg(NO_3)_2$?

12) Potassium cyanide (KCN) is composed of 21.5% nitrogen and 60.1% potassium. How many grams of carbon are in an 82 g sample of KCN.

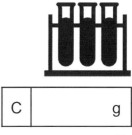

Self-Checking Practice:
Percent Composition (Samples)

Determine the mass percent of the required element in each question. Highlight the correct answer and place the corresponding letter in the row of boxes at the bottom of the page from 1 to 15. A message will appear!

☺	What is the...	The sample contains...	Option 1	Option 2
13	% Na?	9.05 g Na; 13.95 g Cl	46.9% [A]	39.3% [N]
9	% F?	3.72 g Ca; 3.53 g F	48.7% [E]	18.5% [U]
1	% Ca?	4.004 g Ca; 1.199 g C; 4.797 g O	40.04% [P]	24.71% [L]
6	% C?	2.14 g C; 2.86 g O	42.8% [I]	90.2% [A]
10	% Br?	3.12 g Na; 10.87 g Br	37.73% [S]	77.70% [R]
7	% K?	2.72 g K; 3.83 g Mn; 4.45 g O	24.7% [N]	17.4% [L]
2	% H?	1.51 g H; 24.5 g F	1.09% [M]	5.81% [O]
14	% Mg?	3.023 g Mg; 3.977 g S	81.20% [N]	43.19% [T]
5	% Ti?	2.482 g Ti; 5.518 g Cl	31.03% [R]	60.65% [B]
15	% Cl?	0.358 g H; 12.6 g Cl	92.0% [X]	97.2% [S]
11	% O?	1.186 g H; 18.81 g O	94.07% [C]	89.95% [I]
8	% Si?	10.48 g Si; 1.52 g H	12.47% [T]	87.33% [P]
3	% Mn?	4.37 g Mn; 5.63 g Cl	83.4% [M]	43.7% [W]
12	% S?	8.516 g K; 3.485 g S	29.04% [E]	15.98% [A]
4	% P?	2.335 g Li; 3.478 g P; 7.179 g O	26.77% [E]	21.86% [P]

1	2	3	4	5	6	7	8	9	10	11	12	13	14	15

Percent Composition (Using Molar Mass)

We can also calculate percent composition given the <u>chemical formula of a compound</u>. Since there is a fixed proportion of each element in the compound, we can choose a convenient sample size to work from – we will always use ONE MOLE!

This means that we will use the <u>molar masses</u> of each element from the periodic table to complete our calculation.

We follow these steps:

1) Find the <u>molar mass of the compound.</u>
2) Divide <u>the total mass of each element</u> in the compound by the <u>total molar mass</u> and <u>multiply by 100</u> to get the mass percent.
3) Express the mass percent of each element as a <u>percentage</u>.

$$mass\ \%\ element = \frac{(molar\ mass\ of\ element)(\#atoms\ of\ element\ in\ compound)}{molar\ mass\ of\ compound} \times 100\%$$

Example: Find the percent composition of copper (II) sulfate ($CuSO_4$).

1) We start by finding the molar mass of the compound (i.e. the molar mass)

$$M_{CuSO4} = M_{Cu} + M_S + 4 \cdot M_O$$

$$= 63.55 + 32.06 + 4 \cdot 16$$

$$= 159.61\ g/mol$$

2) *We will work through one element at a time:*

$\% \, Cu = \dfrac{63.55}{159.61} \times 100\%$	$\% \, S = \dfrac{32.06}{159.61} \times 100\%$	$\% \, O = \dfrac{4 \cdot 16}{159.61} \times 100\%$
$= 0.398 \times 100\%$	$= 0.201 \times 100\%$	$= 0.401 \times 100\%$
$= 39.8\%$	$= 20.1\%$	$= 40.1\%$

3) ∴ The percent composition of copper (II) sulfate is 39.8% Cu, 20.1% S, and 40.1% O.

Practice: Percent Composition (Molar Mass)

Use the information below to calculate percent composition of each compound below. Round your answers to 1 decimal place.

1) Find the percent composition of methane, CH_4, a primary component of natural gas used for heating. It is also found in cow flatulence!

C	%
H	%

2) Hydrogen peroxide (H_2O_2) is a liquid used as a disinfectant, bleaching agent, and in rocket propulsion. Determine its percent composition.

H	%
O	%

3) Determine the percent composition of sodium chloride (NaCl). It is commonly known as table salt, used a seasoning and preservative in food.

Na	%
Cl	%

Practice: Percent Composition (Molar Mass)

...*continued*

4) While calcium is a shiny silver metal, the compound calcium carbonate ($CaCO_3$) is an important mineral found in bones, rocks, shells, and pearls. What is the mass percent of calcium in calcium carbonate?

Ca	%

5) Ammonia (NH_3) is an important compound in fertilizers and is produced by a reaction known as the Haber process. Determine the percent composition of the compound.

N	%
H	%

6) Glucose ($C_6H_{12}O_6$) is a simple sugar used by the human body in the process of cellular respiration to create energy. It is a product of photosynthesis. What is the mass percent of oxygen in glucose?

O	%

Practice: Percent Composition (Molar Mass)

...continued

7) Find the percent composition of iron (III) oxide (Fe_2O_3), a reddish-brown compound commonly found in rust.

Fe	%
O	%

8) Caffeine ($C_8H_{10}N_4O_2$) is a popular stimulant commonly found in coffee, tea, chocolate, and energy drinks. What is the mass percent of carbon in caffeine?

C	%

9) Sodium bicarbonate ($NaHCO_3$) is commonly known as baking soda. It is a common household item used in baking, cleaning, and more. Find the mass percent of sodium in baking soda.

Na	%

Practice: Percent Composition (Molar Mass)

…continued

10) Hydrogen sulfide (H_2S) is a toxic gas produced during the decay of organic matter in the absence of oxygen, such as in swamps or sewers. It has a "rotten egg" smell. What is the percent composition of hydrogen sulfide?

H	%
S	%

11) Nitroglycerin ($C_3H_5N_3O_9$) is both an explosive compound used in dynamite and a medication used for treating certain heart conditions. What is the mass percent of nitrogen in nitroglycerin?

N	%

12) Hydrochloric acid (HCl) is a strong acid with many industrial and laboratory uses. In high school chemistry, it is often used to teach students about acid-base titrations. What is the percent composition of hydrochloric acid?

H	%
Cl	%

Self-Checking Practice: Percent Composition
(Using Molar Mass)

Determine the mass percent of copper (Cu) in each of the compounds below. <u>Use a ruler</u> to draw a straight line that connects the dot by the compound with the dot by the correct percentage. The line will cross through a number and two letters. Put the letters in the matching numbered box at the bottom of the page. A message will be revealed!

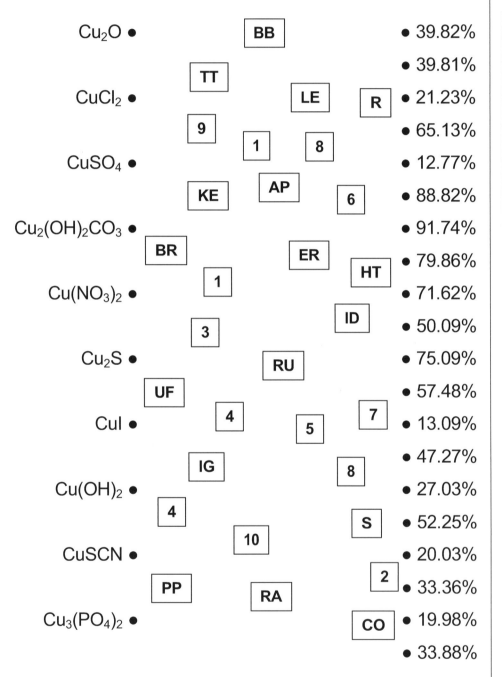

Element	Molar Mass (g/mol)
H	1.01
C	12.01
N	14.01
O	16.00
P	30.97
S	32.06
Cl	35.45
Cu	63.55
I	126.90

Compounds: Cu_2O, $CuCl_2$, $CuSO_4$, $Cu_2(OH)_2CO_3$, $Cu(NO_3)_2$, Cu_2S, CuI, $Cu(OH)_2$, $CuSCN$, $Cu_3(PO_4)_2$

Percentages: 39.82%, 39.81%, 21.23%, 65.13%, 12.77%, 88.82%, 91.74%, 79.86%, 71.62%, 50.09%, 75.09%, 57.48%, 13.09%, 47.27%, 27.03%, 52.25%, 20.03%, 33.36%, 19.98%, 33.88%

1	2	3	4	5	6	7	8	9	10
BR	IG	HT	CO	PP	ER	KE	TT	LE	S

Mixed Practice
Avogadro's Number, Particles, Moles, Molar Mass, Mass, Percent Composition

Answer each question below. Be sure to include the proper number of significant digits in your answer.

1) A chemist is working with 0.025 moles of potassium iodide (KI). How many grams in this?

2) A compound has a mass of 13.0 g. Iodine makes up 7.08 g and chlorine makes up 5.92 g of the sample. What is the percent composition of the compound?

3) How many atoms of beryllium are found in a 1.25 mole sample?

4) Sassolite is the mineral form of boric acid and has the chemical formula of H_3BO_3. What is the mass percent of boron in this compound?

Mixed Practice
Avogadro's Number, Particles, Moles, Molar Mass, Mass, Percent Composition

...continued

5) How many moles are in 37.9 g sample of lead?

6) What is the molar mass of cesium chloride (CsCl)?

7) Vanadium (V) oxide (V_2O_5) is a yellow/brown solid often used in the production of other chemicals. What is the mass percent of vanadium in this compound?

8) What is the mass of 6.02×10^{23} atoms of fluorine?

Empirical Formula vs. Molecular Formula

There are two types of chemical formulas that chemists are interested in:

1. **Empirical Formula**
2. **Molecular Formula**

Empirical Formula: A chemical formula that shows the **simplest whole-number ratio of atoms** present in a compound. It provides insight into the basic composition of a substance, regardless of its molecular structure. It does not always match the actual number of atoms in a molecule.

Molecular Formula: A chemical formula that shows the **actual number of atoms** of each element in a molecule of the compound. It provides information about the composition and structure of the molecule. It always shows us the exact number of atoms in a molecule. The molecular formula is also sometimes called the *true formula.*

Take a look at the table below to see some examples of empirical vs. molecular formulas:

Name of compound	Molecular formula	Lowest ratio of elements		Empirical formula
Cyclobutadiene	C_4H_4	1:1	→	CH
Ethyne	C_2H_2	1:1	→	CH
Benzene	C_6H_6	1:1	→	CH
Glucose	$C_6H_{12}O_6$	1:2:1	→	CH_2O
Formaldehyde	CH_2O	1:2:1	→	CH_2O
Lactic acid	$C_3H_6O_3$	1:2:1	→	CH_2O

Formaldehyde is an example of a case where the empirical formula and the molecular formula are the same.

Practice: Empirical or Molecular Formula?

Look at the chemical formulae below. (Circle) *all the empirical formulae.*

H_2O_2

$C_6H_{12}O_6$

CH_2O

NO_2

P_4O_{10}

Fe_2O_3

C_5H_{11}

$C_{10}H_{22}$

C_2H_6O

HCN

$CHCl_2$

P_2O_5

HF

$C_6H_{18}O_3$

$C_{12}H_{22}O_{11}$

$C_6H_8O_7$

N_2O_4

Na_2SO_4

$NaCl$

MgF_2

Empirical Formula

The **empirical formula** represents the simplest whole-number ratio of atoms of each element present in a compound. It gives us information about the basic composition of a substance.

Questions that ask you to determine the empirical formula often involve first analyzing the *percent composition* of an unknown sample.

We follow these steps:

1) Assume a mass of <u>100.0 g</u> of the sample.
2) Use the <u>percent composition</u> to calculate the mass of each element in a 100.0 g sample.
3) Convert the <u>masses to moles</u> using the molar masses of each element.
4) Determine the simplest whole-number ratio of atoms by <u>dividing each mole value by the smallest mole value.</u>
5) Write the **empirical formula** using these ratios as subscripts for each element.

Example 1: You're given an unknown compound with a percent composition of 40.00% carbon, 6.67% hydrogen, and 53.33% oxygen. It is odourless, has a sweet taste, and is soluble in water.

1) Since the percent composition is the same regardless of how much of the compound we have, we will assume a mass of 100 g to make the calculations as simple as possible.

2) Calculate the masses of each element in the "100 g" sample.

Carbon:	**Hydrogen:**	**Oxygen:**
40.00% = 40.00 g	6.67% = 6.67 g	53.33% = 53.33 g

3) Convert the masses to moles using the molar masses of each element.

Carbon:	**Hydrogen:**	**Oxygen:**
$n_C = \dfrac{40.00}{12.01}$ $= 3.33055787 \dots$ moles	$n_H = \dfrac{6.67}{1.01}$ $= 6.6039604 \dots$ moles	$n_O = \dfrac{53.33}{16.00}$ $= 3.333125 \dots$ moles

4) Determine the simplest whole-number ratio of atoms by dividing each mole value by the smallest mole value. Smallest mole value here is that of carbon (3.33055787…). Remember, don't round until the end!

Carbon:	**Hydrogen:**	**Oxygen:**
$\dfrac{3.33055787 \dots}{3.33055787 \dots} = 1$	$\dfrac{6.6039604 \dots}{3.33055787 \dots} = {\sim}2$	$\dfrac{3.333125 \dots}{3.33055787 \dots} = {\sim}1$

5) Write the empirical formula using the ratios obtained:

$$CH_2O$$

Empirical Formula

Handling Decimal Values

- Don't round too early – it can lead to the wrong answer. You only need to worry about rounding and significant figures at the very end.

- **A note about Step #4** (*Dividing the number of moles of each element by the smallest number of moles obtained*): You'll always get at least one subscript of 1, you won't always end up with a whole number for each subscript. **These decimals will need to be converted to whole numbers** to obtain the empirical formula!

Decimal Value	Multiplier
0.5	2
0.33; 0.66	3
0.25; 0.75	4
0.2; 0.4; 0.6; 0.8	5

Example:
Let's say after dividing the moles of each element by the smallest number of moles, you get this ratio: $C_{1.5}H_3O_1$

To convert all subscripts to whole numbers, multiply each subscript by 2 to end up with: $C_3H_6O_2$

Example 2: The percent composition of a hydrocarbon is 81.7% carbon and 18.3% hydrogen. What is its empirical formula?

1) We'll assume a mass of 100 g to make the calculations as simple as possible.

2) Calculate the masses of each element in the "100 g" sample.

Carbon:	**Hydrogen:**
81.7% = 81.7 g	18.3% = 18.3 g

3) Convert the masses to moles using the molar masses of each element.

Carbon:	**Hydrogen:**
$n_C = \dfrac{81.7}{12.01}$ $= 6.802664\ldots$ moles	$n_H = \dfrac{18.3}{1.01}$ $= 18.11881188\ldots$ moles

4) Determine the simplest whole-number ratio of atoms by dividing each mole value by the smallest mole value. Smallest mole value here is that of carbon (6.802664...)

Carbon:	**Hydrogen:**
$\dfrac{6.802664\ldots}{6.802664\ldots} = 1$	$\dfrac{18.11881188\ldots}{6.802664\ldots} = {\sim}2.66$

Since 2.66 isn't a whole number, we compare its decimals to the table to find the right multiplier. It doesn't have to be exactly the same as the table, but it should be really close! In this case, we multiply by 3.

5) Multiply each subscript by 3 (based on the table at the top of the page). Write the empirical formula using the adjusted subscript.

$$C_3H_8$$

Practice: Empirical Formula

Use the information below to determine the empirical formula of each compound described below.

1) A highly exothermic reaction between phosphorus and oxygen gas results in the formation of a white, crystalline powder. The compound is composed of 43.7% phosphorus and 56.4% oxygen. What is the empirical formula of the compound?

2) A compound appears as bright orange crystals and is commonly used in various industrial applications, including the production of pigments. The compound is composed of 17.6% sodium, 39.7% chromium, and 42.8% oxygen. What is the empirical formula of the compound?

Practice: Empirical Formula

...continued

3) A compound contains 69.9% iron and 30.1% oxygen. What is the empirical formula of this compound?

4) A compound is made up of 64.63% nitrogen, and the rest is sodium. Find its empirical formula.

Practice: Empirical Formula

5) Vitamin C is made up of 40.81% carbon, 4.57% hydrogen, and 54.62% oxygen. What is the empirical formula of vitamin C?

6) A compound is composed of 39.67% potassium, 27.87% manganese, and 32.46% oxygen. What is its empirical formula?

Practice: Empirical Formula

...continued

7) A major textile dye manufacturer developed a new yellow dye. The dye has a percent composition of 75.95% C, 17.72% N, and 6.33% H by mass. What is its empirical formula?

 After dividing the mole values by the smallest mole value, a general rule is that you can round your subscript up when it is bigger than x.95 or down when it is less than x.05.

8) Caffeine has the following percent composition: carbon 49.48%, hydrogen 5.19%, oxygen 16.48% and nitrogen 28.85%. What is the empirical formula?

Practice: Empirical Formula

…continued

9) A sample of an unknown compound has been analyzed and results show that is composed of 87.3 g of sodium, 121.5 g of sulfur, and 91.2 grams of oxygen. Determine its empirical formula.

10) A mystery compound is determined to be composed of 73.6 g of nitrogen and 126.4 g of oxygen. Determine its empirical formula.

Self-Checking Practice:
Empirical Formula

Find the empirical formula of the compound described below. Then, follow the instructions based on the subscripts to check your answer.

Fun fact! This compound is found only in aqueous form, and its decomposition is an important reaction related to the formation of geological formations in caves including stalactites and stalagmites.

Element	Mass Percent
Calcium (Ca)	24.7%
Hydrogen (H)	1.25%
Carbon (C)	14.75%
Oxygen (O)	59.3%

Element	Find your subscript...						Your answer is correct if you see...
	1	2	3	4	5	6	
Ca	Go to p.31	Go to p.43	Go to p.37	Go to p.62	Go to p.25	Go to p.27	
H	Go to p.55	Go to p.15	Go to p.62	Go to p.27	Go to p.37	Go to p.66	
C	Go to p.66	Go to p.25	Go to p.31	Go to p.15	Go to p.62	Go to p.46	
O	Go to p.62	Go to p.41	Go to p.27	Go to p.10	Go to p.66	Go to p.72	

Molecular Formula

The **molecular formula** is the chemical formula that shows the **actual number of atoms** of each element in a molecular compound. It provides information about the composition and structure of the molecule.

Determining the identify of a compound is important in all kinds of research. As we have seen, the empirical formula alone doesn't always allow us to identify a compound.

We follow these steps:

1) Calculate the molar mass of the empirical formula.
2) Obtain the experimental molar mass of the unknown compound.
3) Calculate the "multiplier" by dividing the experimental molar mass by the molar mass of the empirical formula.
4) Multiply the subscripts in the empirical formula by the multiplier.
5) Write the **molecular formula** using the new subscripts for each element.

Example: Further testing is done on the odourless, sweet-tasting, water-soluble compound from the *Empirical Formula section* and the mass spectrometry results show that it has a molar mass of 180.18 g/mol. Its empirical formula is CH_2O. What is its molecular formula?

1) Calculate the molar mass of the empirical formula.

$$M_{CH2} - M_C + 2 \cdot M_H + M_O$$

$$= 12.01 + 2 \cdot 1.01 + 16.00$$

$$= 30.03 \text{ g/mol}$$

2) The experimental molar mass of the unknown compound is **180.18 g**.

3) Calculate the "multiplier" by dividing the experimental molar mass by the molar mass of the empirical formula.

$$Multiplier = 180.18 \div 30.03$$

$$= 6$$

5) Multiply the subscripts in the empirical formula (CH_2O) by the multiplier.

$$C_{1 \cdot 6}H_{2 \cdot 6}O_{1 \cdot 6}$$

5) Write the molecular formula using the new subscripts for each element:

$$C_6H_{12}O_6$$

Practice: Molecular Formula

Use the information below to determine the molecular formula of each compound described below.

1) The empirical formula of a compound is NO_2, and the substance has a molar mass of 92.02 g/mol. What is the molecular formula?

2) The empirical formula of a compound is C_5H_9 and the molar mass is 345.70 g/mol. What is the molecular formula of the compound?

Practice: Molecular Formula

...continued

3) The empirical formula for a toxic, colorless, and pyrophoric gas with a repulsively sweet odor is BH_3. It has a molar mass of 27.68 g/mol. What is the molecular formula?

4) A hydrocarbon has the empirical formula of CH_2 and a molar mass of 70.15 g/mol. What is the molecular formula?

5) The empirical formula of a compound was determined to be CH. If the molar mass is known to be 78.12 g/mol, what is the molecular formula?

6) Triethylenemelamine is an odorless white powder with an empirical formula of $C_3H_4N_2$ and a molar mass of 204.27 g/mol. Determine its molecular formula.

Practice: Molecular Formula

…continued

7) A common form of asbestos has an empirical formula of $Mg_3Si_2H_3O_8$ and a molar mass of 520.28 g/mol. What is the molecular formula of this compound?

8) A compound is composed of 74.83% carbon and 25.17% hydrogen and has a molar mass of 16.05 g/mol. What is its molecular formula?

Practice: Molecular Formula

...continued

9) Determine the molecular formula of a compound that is composed of 74.98% carbon, 5.04% hydrogen, and 19.98% oxygen. It has a molar mass of 240.27 g/mol.

10) An unknown compound is a colorless liquid with a burnt match smell. It is composed of 25.232% sulfur. The remainder of the compound is fluorine. Analysis shows that the molar mass of the compound is 254.12 g/mol. What is the molecular formula of the compound?

Self-Checking Practice: Molecular Formula

Determine the molecular formula of each compound given its empirical formula and molar mass. Highlight the correct answer and place the corresponding letters in the blank spaces at the bottom of the page from 1 to 8. A message will appear!

#	Empirical Formula of Compound	Molar Mass of Compound (g/mol)	Option 1	Option 2
6	CH_2	70	C_5H_{10} [IO]	$C_{10}H_{20}$ [AO]
2	N_2O_5	108.0	$N_{10}O_{25}$ [CU]	N_2O_5 [BR]
8	C_3H_3O	110	C_3H_3O [ST]	$C_6H_6O_2$ [TY]
1	C_2H_4O	88	$C_6H_{12}O_3$ [SE]	$C_4H_8O_2$ [EM]
4	OCNCl	232.41	$O_3C_3N_3Cl_3$ [EC]	$O_4C_4N_4Cl_4$ [CD]
7	NO_2	92	N_2O_4 [SI]	N_4O_8 [KA]
5	N_2O_3	152	N_2O_3	N_4O_6 [UR]
3	P_2O_5	238.88	P_4O_{10} [AC]	P_6O_{15} [DR]

Element	Molar Mass (g/mol)
H	1.01
C	12.01
N	14.01
O	16.00
P	30.97
S	32.06
Cl	35.45
Cu	63.55
I	126.90

1   2   3   4   5   6   7   8

Mixed Practice
Avogadro's Number, Particles, Moles, Molar Mass, Mass, Percent Composition, Empirical Formula, Molecular Formula

Answer each question below. Be sure to include the proper number of significant digits in your answer.

1) A chemist is working with 2.5 mol of silicon dioxide (SiO_2). How many atoms are in this sample?

2) Determine the empirical formula of a compound made up of 73.02% fluorine and 26.98% silicon.

3) How many moles are in a 5.4 g sample of magnesium oxide (MgO)?

4) What is the mass percent of titanium in $TiBr_2$?

Mixed Practice
Avogadro's Number, Particles, Moles, Molar Mass, Mass, Percent Composition, Empirical Formula, Molecular Formula

...continued

5) 1,4-dichlorobutane is a colorless liquid that can be used as a precursor for nylon. It has the molecular formula of $C_4H_8Cl_2$. What is its empirical formula?

6) What is the molar mass of rubidium phosphide (Rb_3P)?

7) What is the mass percent of phosphorus in phosphorus trichloride (PCl_3)?

8) A molecule has a molar mass of 84.12 g/mol and an empirical formula of CH_2N. What is the molecular formula?

Mixed Practice
Avogadro's Number, Particles, Moles, Molar Mass, Mass, Percent Composition, Empirical Formula, Molecular Formula

…continued

9) What is the mass of a sample of ammonia (NH_3) that contains 7.25 moles?

10) How many formula units are in 0.095 mol of calcium bromide ($CaBr_2$)?

11) How many atoms are in 0.095 mol of calcium bromide ($CaBr_2$)?

12) What is the percent composition of calcium bromide ($CaBr_2$)?

SOLUTIONS

Solutions

Self-Checking Practice: Significant Digits
(p. 8)

Answer: In science, even failure leads to discovery

Self-Checking Practice: Doing Math with Significant Digits
(p. 10)

Answer: RAIN

Practice: Moles and Avogadro's Number
(p. 14)

1) 9.42 moles
2) 0.467 moles
3) 19.9 moles
4) 0.000075 moles
5) 0.0884 moles
6) 0.0311 moles
7) 0.00520 moles
8) 0.000638 moles
9) 0.0450 moles
10) 2,240,000 moles

Practice: Particles and Avogadro's Number
(p. 16)

1) 7.2×10^{23} formula units
2) 1.5×10^{24} atoms
3) 4.5×10^{23} molecules
4) 1.5×10^{23} molecules
5) 4.5×10^{23} atoms
6) 1.4×10^{24} formula units
7) 2.8×10^{24} chloride ions
8) 2.4×10^{23} atoms
9) 1.5×10^{24} molecules
10) 4.3×10^{23} atoms

Self-Checking Practice: Moles, Particles, and Avogadro's Number
(p. 18)

Answer: The letter K

Solutions

...*continued*

Self-Checking Practice: Calculating Molar Mass
(p. 20)

Answer: MATTER

Practice: Moles, Mass, and Molar Mass (Part A)
(p. 24)

1) 0.974 moles
2) 13.09 moles
3) 0.197 moles
4) 33.02 moles
5) 0.590 moles
6) 12.34 moles
7) 1.3 moles
8) 0.305 moles
9) 0.0431 moles
10) 17.22 moles

Practice: Moles, Mass, and Molar Mass (Part B)
(p. 26)

1) 110 g
2) 70. g
3) 41.3 g
4) 182.7 g
5) 199 g
6) 135 g
7) 10,800 g
8) 105 g
9) 3598 g
10) 0.041 g

Self-Checking Practice: Moles, Mass, and Molar Mass
(p. 28)

Answer: PERIODIC

Solutions

...continued

Mixed Practice: Avogadro's Number, Particles, Moles, Molar Mass, Mass
(p. 30)

1) 290 g
2) 7.498×10^{-9} moles
3) 1.03×10^{23} atoms
4) 0.086 moles
5) 1.6×10^{22} molecules
6) 128.2 g/mol
7) 132 g
8) 3.03 moles
9) 162.26 g/mol
10) 150 g

Practice: Percent Composition (Samples)
(p. 34)

1) Cu: 28.4%; Br: 71.6%
2) H: 3.0%; Cl: 97%
3) K: 52.45%; Cl: 47.55%
4) Fe: 46.82%; P: 17.29%; O: 35:89%
5) O: 27.5 g; O: 47.4%
6) Mg: 28.8%; C: 14%; O: 57.0%
7) N: 82.1%
8) Zn: 67.10%; S: 32.90%
9) Cl: 89.1%
10) N: 60.9 g
11) Mg: 7.38 g
12) C: 15 g

Self-Checking Practice: Percent Composition (Samples)
(p. 38)

Answer: Power in percents

Practice: Percent Composition (Molar Mass)
(p. 40)

1) C: 74.8%; H: 25.2%
2) H: 5.9%; O: 94.1%
3) Na: 39.3%; Cl: 60.7%
4) Ca: 40.0%
5) N: 82.2%; H: 17.8%
6) O: 53.3%
7) Fe: 69.9%; O: 30.1%
8) C: 49.5%
9) Na: 27.4%
10) H: 5.9%; S: 94.1%
11) N: 18.5%
12) H: 2.8%; Cl: 97.2%

Solutions

...*continued*

<u>**Self-Checking Practice: Percent Composition (Molar Mass)**</u>
<u>**(p. 44)**</u>

Answer: BRIGHT COPPER KETTLES

<u>**Mixed Practice: Avogadro's Number, Particles, Moles, Molar Mass, Mass, Percent Composition**</u>
<u>**(p. 45)**</u>

1) 4.2 g
2) I: 54.5%; Cl: 45.5%
3) 7.53×10^{23} atoms
4) B: 17.5%
5) 0.183 moles
6) 168.36 g/mol
7) %V: 56.0%
8) 19 g

<u>**Practice: Empirical or Molecular Formula?**</u>
<u>**(p. 48)**</u> ➡

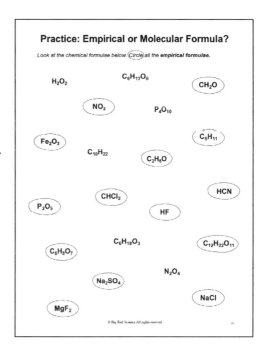

<u>**Practice: Empirical Formula**</u>
<u>**(p. 51)**</u>

1) P_2O_5
2) $Na_2Cr_2O_7$
3) Fe_2O_3
4) NaN_3
5) $C_3H_4O_3$
6) K_2MnO_4
7) C_5H_5N
8) $C_4H_5N_2O$
9) $Na_2S_2O_3$
10) N_2O_3

<u>**Self-Checking Practice: Empirical Formula**</u>
<u>**(p. 56)**</u>

Answer: $CaH_2C_2O_6$

Solutions

...continued

Practice: Molecular Formula
(p. 58)

1) N_2O_4
2) $C_{25}H_{45}$
3) B_2H_6
4) C_5H_{10}
5) C_6H_6
6) $C_9H_{12}N_6$
7) $Mg_6Si_4H_6O_{16}$
8) CH_4
9) $C_{15}H_{12}O_3$
10) S_2F_{10}

Self-Checking Practice: Molecular Formula
(p. 63)

Answer: EMBRACE CURIOSITY

Mixed Practice: Avogadro's Number, Particles, Moles, Molar Mass, Mass, Percent Composition, Empirical Formula, and Molecular Formula
(p. 64)

1) 4.5×10^{24} atoms
2) SiF_4
3) 0.13 moles
4) Ti: 23.05%
5) C_2H_4Cl
6) 287.38 g/mol
7) 22.55%
8) $C_3H_6N_3$
9) 124 g
10) 5.7×10^{22} formula units
11) 1.7×10^{23} atoms
12) Cu: 20.05%

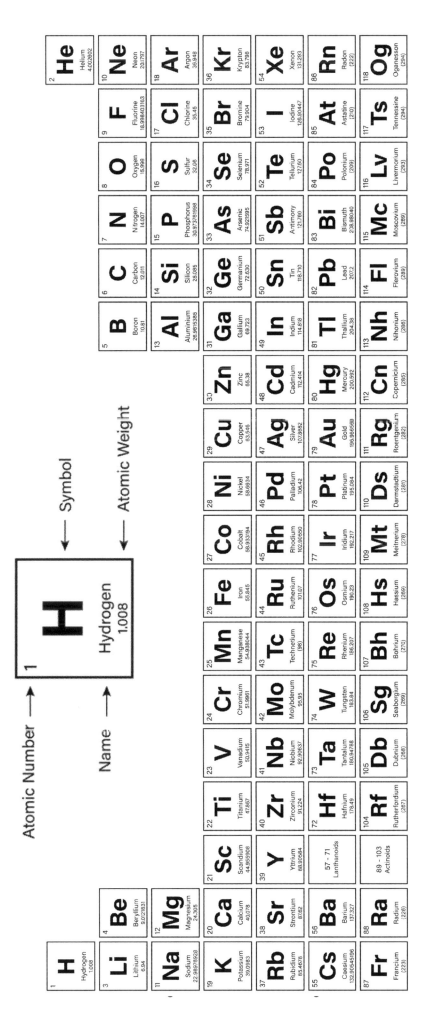

Reference Tables

This table shows some of the common molar masses that you will be working with in this workbook. All of these values can also be found on the Periodic Table of Elements on pg. 73, along with the molar mass of any other element not listed here.

Common Molar Masses		
Atomic Number	Element	Molar Mass (g/mol)
1	Hydrogen	1.01
3	Lithium	6.94
5	Boron	10.81
6	Carbon	12.01
7	Nitrogen	14.01
8	Oxygen	16.00
9	Fluorine	19.00
11	Sodium	23.00
12	Magnesium	24.31
13	Aluminum	26.98
14	Silicon	28.09
15	Phosphorus	30.97
16	Sulfur	32.06
17	Chlorine	35.45
19	Potassium	39.10
20	Calcium	40.08
26	Iron	55.85
29	Copper	63.55
35	Bromine	79.90
47	Silver	107.87
53	Iodine	126.90

Reference Tables

Common Multivalent Metals

Metal	Element Symbol	Ion Symbols	Ion names
Cobalt	Co	Co^{2+} Co^{3+}	Cobalt (II) Cobalt (III)
Chromium	Cr	Cr^{2+} Cr^{3+}	Chromium (II) Chromium (III)
Copper	Cu	Cu^{+} Cu^{2+}	Copper(I) Copper(II)
Iron	Fe	Fe^{2+} Fe^{3+}	Iron (II) Iron (III)
Lead	Pb	Pb^{2+} Pb^{4+}	Lead (II) Lead (IV)
Manganese	Mn	Mn^{2+} Mn^{4+}	Manganese (II) Manganese (IV)
Mercury	Hg	Hg^{+} Hg^{2+}	Mercury (I) Mercury (II)
Tin	Sn	Sn^{2+} Sn^{4+}	Tin (II) Tin (IV)
Titanium	Ti	Ti^{3+} Ti^{4+}	Titanium (III) Titanium (IV)
Vanadium	V	V^{3+} V^{5+}	Vanadium (III) Vanadium (V)

Common Polyatomic Ions

Name	Ion	Name	Ion
Acetate	$C_2H_3O^-$	Hydroxide	OH^-
Ammonium	NH_4^+	Hypochlorite	ClO^-
Bicarbonate	HCO_3^-	Nitrate	NO_3^-
Bromate	BrO_3^-	Nitrite	NO_2^-
Carbonate	CO_3^{2-}	Perchlorate	ClO_4^-
Chlorate	ClO_3^-	Permanganate	MnO_4^-
Chlorite	ClO_2^-	Phosphate	PO_4^{3-}
Chromate	CrO_4^{2-}	Phosphite	PO_3^{3-}
Cyanide	CN^-	Sulfate	SO_4^{2-}
Dichromate	$Cr_2O_7^{2-}$	Sulfite	SO_3^{2-}

Reference Tables

Common Acids	
Name	**Chemical Formula**
Acetic acid	$HC_2H_3O_2$
Bromic acid	$HBrO_3$
Carbonic acid	H_2CO_3
Chlorous acid	$HClO_2$
Hydrobromic acid	HBr
Hydrochloric acid	HCl
Hydrocyanic acid	HCN
Hydrofluoric acid	HF
Hydroiodic acid	HI
Hydrosulfuric acid	H_2S
Hypobromous acid	HBrO
Hypochlorous acid	HClO
Hypoiodous acid	HIO
Iodic acid	HIO_3
Nitric acid	HNO_3
Nitrous acid	HNO_2
Perbromic acid	$HBrO_4$
Perchloric acid	$HClO_4$
Periodic acid	HIO_4
Phosphoric acid	H_3PO_4
Sulfuric acid	H_2SO_4
Sulfurous acid	H_2SO_3

Reference Tables

The Activity Series (Metals)

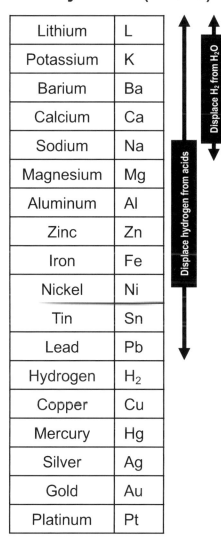

Lithium	L
Potassium	K
Barium	Ba
Calcium	Ca
Sodium	Na
Magnesium	Mg
Aluminum	Al
Zinc	Zn
Iron	Fe
Nickel	Ni
Tin	Sn
Lead	Pb
Hydrogen	H_2
Copper	Cu
Mercury	Hg
Silver	Ag
Gold	Au
Platinum	Pt

Displace H_2 from H_2O

Displace hydrogen from acids

The Activity Series (Halogens)

Fluorine	F_2
Chlorine	Cl_2
Bromine	Br_2
Iodine	I_2

Reference Tables

The Solubility Rules

Soluble Compounds	Exceptions
Alkali metal (Group IA) compounds (Li^+, Na^+, K^+, Cs^+, Rb^+)	None
Ammonium (NH_4^+) compounds	None
Nitrates (NO_3^-) Acetates (CH_3COO^-) Chlorates (ClO_3^-), Perchlorates (ClO_4^-)	None
Chlorides (Cl^-) Bromides (Br^-) Iodides (I^-)	Exceptions: Ag^+, Cu^+, Hg_2^{2+}, and Pb^{2+} compounds are insoluble.
Sulfates (SO_4^{2-})	Exception: Ag^+, Ba^{2+}, Ca^{2+}, Hg_2^{2+}, and Pb^{2+} compounds are insoluble.
Insoluble Compounds	**Exceptions**
Hydroxides (OH^-)	Exceptions: Alkali metal hydroxides, $Ba(OH)_2$, and $Ca(OH)_2$ are soluble.
Carbonates (CO_3^{2-}) Phosphates (PO_4^{3-})	Exceptions: Alkali metal and NH_4^+ compounds are soluble.
Sulfides (S^{2-})	Exceptions: Alkali metal, Alkaline Earth metal, and NH_4^+ compounds are soluble.

Want a **FREE** resource to help you master chemical reactions?

47292301R00043